All Kids Are Loved

Who made all the kids cry? Why? We'll find out and make them happy again!

"Hey buddies, why's everyone crying? What's wrong"

Set 10 - Book 5

Berkeley Boys Books

Vaughn Berkeley
(Guest Author of the Berkeley Boys Book Series)

All Kids Are Loved (Berkeley Boys Books)

By: Vaughn Berkeley

Print ISBN: 978-1-989612-94-1

Published by C.M. Berkeley Media Group

www.cmberkeleymediagroup.com

Copyright© 2025 by Vaughn Berkeley. All rights reserved. Without limiting the rights under copyright reserved above, no part of this publication may be reproduced, stored in or introduced into a retrieval system, or transmitted, in any form, or by any means (electronic, mechanical, photocopying, recording, or otherwise) without the prior written permission of both the copyright owner and the above publisher of this book. Any resemblance to characters, places, brands, media, and incidents are purely coincidental. The author acknowledges the trademarked status and trademark owners of various products referenced in this work, which have been used without permission. The publication/use of these trademarks is not authorized, associated with, or sponsored by the trademark owners.

Digital Edition License Notes

The digital version of this book is licensed for your individual personal enjoyment only. This digital book may not be re-sold or given away to other people. If you would like to share this book with another person, please purchase an additional copy for each person you share it with. If you're reading this book and did not purchase it, or it was not purchased for your use only, then you should return to your online e-book retailer or the author's website and purchase your own copy. Thank you for respecting the author's work.

All Kids Are Loved (Berkeley Boys Books)
Other Great Books

Grab these titles at Amazon, Barnes and Noble and other major online book sellers.

Vaughn Berkeley
Other Great Books

Grab these titles at Amazon, Barnes and Noble and other major online book sellers.

All Kids Are Loved (Berkeley Boys Books)

Other Great Books

Grab these titles at Amazon, Barnes and Noble and other major online book sellers.

Vaughn Berkeley

Other Great Books

Get them all at major online book sellers today!

All Kids Are Loved (Berkeley Boys Books)

Other Great Books

  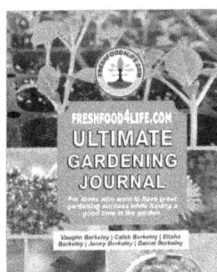 

Grab these titles at Amazon, Barnes and Noble and other major online book sellers.

Place your
photo here.

Name:
_____

Age:
_____

City:
_____

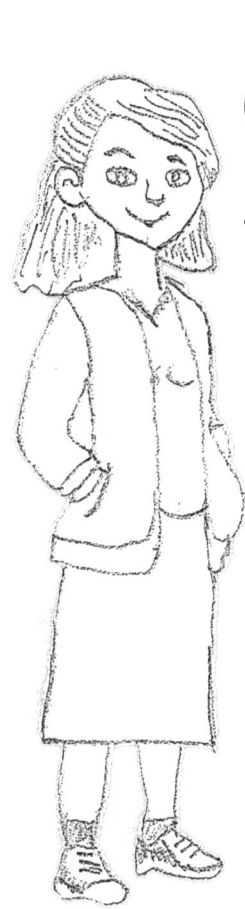

Ashley is a white girl

Timmy is a brown boy

Alasie is an aboriginal boy

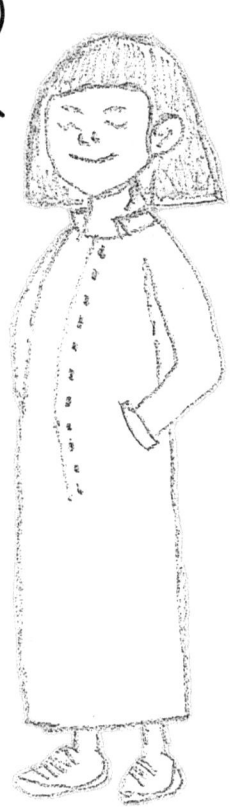

Ching is a Chinese girl

They are best friends and kind to each other

They play and have fun together

Their parents and teachers teach them the right way

The 10 Commandments
1. Love God With All Your Heart
2. Don't Worship Idols
3. Don't Dishonor God's Name
4. Remember Sabbath
5. Honor Your Parents
6. Don't Kill People
7. Don't Steal
8. Don't Break Marriages
9. Don't Lie On Others
10. Don't Want Your Neighbor's House, Wife, Servants, Ox, Donkey or Anything That Belongs To Your Neighbor

They love each other because of their upright character

They speak out against racism, tyranny, or oppression

Vaughn Berkeley

They want people to be kind and compassionate

God (Yah) loves these upright children

They are happy, content, and loved

The End

New words we learned today!

1. white
2. girl
3. brown
4. boy
5. aboriginal
6. chinese
7. best
8. friends
9. play
10. laugh
11. racism
12. kind
13. content
14. upright
15. tyranny
16. loved

It's time for a MAZE!!

Word Scrambles

IGLR _ _ _ _

OBNRW _ _ _ _ _

YBO _ _ _

INLGIOABRA _ _ _ _ _ _ _ _ _

ENISHCE _ _ _ _ _ _ _

TBES _ _ _ _

NFRDIES _ _ _ _ _ _ _

AYPL _ _ _ _

HLGAU _ _ _ _ _

SMICAR _ _ _ _ _ _

NIDK _ _ _ _

TETNCNO _ _ _ _ _ _ _

Word Searches

Vaughn Berkeley

```
K H C I N W O R B S F S L V V
J Y L O V E D U Z L D A D A M
S I N I M F U L P N O X N C L
N P E N A P C W E R H X I X B
I W S Y A V R I W B I A K E O
I F G O L R R F C A B G S M W
R U U B R F Y K R O W T H E O
A G Z F C D W T R G N J G T R
C F X C A X U I C L M T P E G
I H J O K W G H A V I L E I R
S T G G W I I U H W A H R N G
M F P W N N G A S Y H L P A T
M A E A E H S B I U R I U M C
T K L S F C I D Y U F C T W U
U W E F D H O X Z S E R N E Q
```

white   best   content
girl   friends   upright
brown   play   tyranny
boy   laugh   loved
aboriginal   racism
chinese   kind

About Vaughn Berkeley

Vaughn Berkeley is loving husband and dedicated father. He's a writing coach, author of numerous books and articles over a 25+ year timeframe. Vaughn was co-publisher of a health and wellness magazine in Toronto for close to a decade. Vaughn's an online course creator, a branding/website design consultant, and a lifelong supporter of the poor and working poor. Vaughn is also a gardener, and a man on a spiritual quest. He is the patriarch of a family of authors who have jointly written or co-written more than 100 books!

When Vaughn is not busy behind the computer consulting remotely with a client in Toronto or the Caribbean, he can be found spending time in his garden or taking photographs on the hiking trails nearby. Vaughn motto: Living a life of worth!

Find out more or reach out to Vaughn for help at:
vaughnberkeley.com

About the Berkeley Boys

Caleb Berkeley is a published author since he was 7 years old. He is an author of over 100 books, YouTuber, video editor, video script writer, scripture card game creator, graphic editor, artist, and loving son and big brother. He's polite, kind, quiet, and capable. He is a product of the Montessori school.

Elisha Berkeley is an author following his brother. His first book was published at the age of 7. Elisha is currently an author of over 80 books. Elisha created easy reader books, a planner, writing books, and learning books for kids. Elisha is also a product of Montessori school. He's loves gardening and is a loving son and brother.

Find out more or reach out to them at:
https://linktr.ee/berkeleys

Answers to the Puzzles

IGLR = GIRL

OBNRW = BROWN

YBO = BOY

INLGIOABRA = ABORIGINAL

ENISHCE = CHINESE

TBES = BEST

NFRDIES = FRIENDS

AYPL = PLAY

HLGAU = LAUGH

SMICAR = RACISM

NIDK = KIND

TETNCNO = CONTENT

Grab all of set 5 today at major online bookstores

More from CM Berkeley Media Group

CM Berkeley Media Group, based in Canada, works with its authors to produce books which help to uplift the human spirit, spread the message of health and wellness, and offer practical insights in finances, and other areas.

Website: cmberkeleymediagroup.com

Grab these other great titles at Amazon worldwide and other major online booksellers.

For Adults
- Break The Poverty Curse: Unlock Your Prosperity 2026 & 2027 Success Planner - School of Prophets Edition
(A Great tool for 17 to 70. This contains more info to help structure your life spiritually and in this life. It is produced every 2 years - new edition comes out Fall 2023, 2025, 2027, and so on)
- Break The Poverty Curse: Unlock Your Prosperity (2017 Edition)
- Break The Poverty Curse: Unlock Your Prosperity - Puzzle Power 1
- Break The Poverty Curse: Unlock Your Prosperity - Puzzle Power 2
- Break The Poverty Curse: Unlock Your Prosperity - Puzzle Power 3
- Break The Poverty Curse: Unlock Your Prosperity - CRASH PROOF (coming soon)
- Jenny's 99 Health Quotes To Empower Your Life
- Eating4Eternity: Unlock Your Holistic Health Lifestyle. Sweet Raw Desserts: Life Is Sweet Raw™
- Can I Offer You A Cigarette: The Only Sure Way To Break The Smoking Habit
- Colon By Design: Overcoming The Stigma Of Colon Sickness And Unlocking True Colon Health™
- Fresh Food4Life™: The Case For Taking Back Control of Your Food And Empowering Your Family And Community.
- FreshFood4Life.com Ultimate Gardening Journal
- Seeking His Presence (coming soon)

All Kids Are Loved (Berkeley Boys Books)

For Teens and Young Adults

The Youth Leadership Empowerment System™

Jump into the world of Dr Vicktor Maximitas, world famous psychologist by day and legendary demon hunter by night. Go into this mystery world where good triumphs over evil and souls are rescued from demonic clutches.

- A Maximitas Novel: Unholy Fyre (Book 1)
- A Maximitas Novel: Unholy Fyre (Book 2)

For Children

The Adventures of Moshe Monkey and Elias Froggy book series.

- The Adventures of Moshe Monkey and Elias Froggy: A Healthy Business (Volume 1)
- Moshe and Elias Build A Garden (The Adventures of Moshe Monkey and Elias Froggy) (Volume 2)
- Moshe and Elias Tropical Vacation (The Adventures of Moshe Monkey and Elias Froggy) (Volume 3)
- Living Foods for Boys and Girls (The Adventures of Moshe Monkey and Elias Froggy) (Volume 4)
- Moshe Monkey Breaks His Leg (The Adventures of Moshe Monkey and Elias Froggy) (Volume 5)
- Moshe Monkey And Elias Froggy: Puzzle Book (1 to 9)
- Fun with your ABC's
- The Amazing Colouring and Learning Book of Fruits and Veggies
- School of the Prophets for Children Planner - Ultimate Edition
- Moshe Monkey And Elias Froggy - Daily Journal
- Baldy's Life
- Baldy's Writing Book for New Words
- Berkeley Short Stories, Doodles and Writing Prompts
- Berkeley Short Stories, Doodles and Writing Prompts 2
- Scripture Brain Power 1
- Scripture Brain Power 2
- Roll the Ball
- Mom and Dad
- Ann Can Count To 10
- My Easy Cursive Handwriting Book
- Bounce the Ball

- Mow the Lawn
- Mouzzie Goes Home (Mouzzie Mouse Adventures) (Book 1)

The El Caldani Missions series of books are designed for first readers to help learn their ABC's and basic skills with each book. Titles include:
- El Caldani Discovers A Words
- El Caldani Discovers B Words
- El Caldani Discovers C Words

All the way through to Z words

Other El Caldani Titles includes
- El Caldani Discovers Shapes
- El Caldani Discovers Squares
- El Caldani Discovers Circles
- El Caldani Discovers Addition
- El Caldani Discovers Subtraction
- And many more

The El Caldani Missions series is a comprehensive series to help walk your young child through various fundamental aspects of education. Grab the entire set for your child or student today. You'll be glad you did!

Plus there are many more books to entertain new readers while teaching them about important life lessons.

* * * * *

Check out these titles on Amazon and major online book sellers.

www.ingramcontent.com/pod-product-compliance
Lightning Source LLC
Chambersburg PA
CBHW071400090426
42736CB00015B/3209